NATURAL LIFE

NATURAL LIFE

A POETIC FIELD GUIDE

STANLEY KUSUNOKI

NODIN PRESS

ISBN:1-978-847237-70-4
Library of Congress Control Number: 2025946684
Cover design: James Monroe Design
Book design: John Toren

Published by Nodin Press
218 Edge Place
Minneapolis, MN 55418

Printed in USA

To My wife,muse, and heartbeat, Claudia;
and to all who fight for the Natural Life of the planet.

Contents

Flora and Fauna

Earth and Sky

Homo Sapiens

Wee Poems from Skye

Fresh Sightings

FLORA AND FAUNA

Autumn Leaves

Autumn leaves
It leaves too soon
This dit of time
from summer's swelter
to whirling snows of winter

This year we fear time
ever more fleeting
Drought, scorching sun
in the west and north,
new color palette
mostly brown
relieved by a few paltry hot pink
tamarisk fronds.

Coneflowers dusty.
Meteorologists muse
on the changing foliage
while we anxiously watch
the crowns of aspen
for sunlight gold,
flickering crimson tongues
of flame on maple and sumac,
we yearn to soak in all the colors.
Store it all like a bulb,
deep in memory

Blooming in Place

Outside
The hibiscus leafs out
in the sun of July and August,
Basks without blooming
"Just chillin'" it drawls.

We try not to be impatient,
coaxing with Miracle Grow,
cajoling it with competitive spite.
"Man, what a great year for basil!
And look at the rosemary and lavender!"
Even the Anaheim peppers
put out a bumper crop

The hibiscus is not impressed.
Just stretches, yawns, leaves
reaching upward like green palms.
"Just not in the mood
Don't bug me."
"Have it your way" we say,
benign neglect.
Like watering only once a week
while deadheading petunias
and geraniums.

But soon the annuals wither
The peppers are all picked
and the herbs pulled out and dried.
Stalks are chopped, leaves are raked
and piled into black bags
off to the composting center

And the hibiscus
moves indoors
shut-in away
from the world outside
The noisy annuals gone

It blooms with abandon

Crime Scene

1. **The evidence:**

– Massive guano splats have appeared on the windshield and rear quarter panel of the grey Saturn parked in the alley

– Grey, black and white feathers dust the passenger window and windshield of the Saturn

– Crimson feather lies by the gate

– Blood trails in the melting snow

Inspector's hypothesis:

– Victims were likely a slate-colored junco and juvenile cardinal
– Guano splatter patterns and distribution of feathers suggest a hit in flight
– Prime suspect, a rough-legged hawk seen recently near the crime scene, or another predator large enough to fly off with its victims

Course of Action:

– Maintain vigilance over the crime scene
– Seek corroborating evidence
Update: The evidence is disappearing
Blood trail erased by melting snow
Feathers dusted off by the custodian winds

Guano splatter pattern lost at the car wash
Greedy red squirrel now in witness protection
Absence of chickadee chatter
Killer still at large

2. Weekly Update

Wildlife steering clear of the crime scene
No takers at the bird feeder
but a pair of mourning doves
lunches under the bird bath
Have they been on vacation? Did no one tell
them of the violence right here
where they peck at seeds and nuts?

3. Weekly Update

It has been a month
Crime unsolved
Feeder stays full day after day
No sightings of the perpetrator

4. Weekly Update

One squirrel
A chickadee
The all clear goes out via blue jay bullhorn
cardinals tweet, sparrows twitter.
Flutters of activity. Crime unsolved, but we venture out

Day Trip to NYC

Saw-whet owl
bored with the scenery
in the Saugerties,
thought he'd take in
the Big Apple.
Hitched a ride
on a Norway spruce.
Just wanted to see the sights—
Times Square,
The Statue.
Didn't plan on being
A cause célèbres—
Man, Rockefeller Plaza,
the iconic tree--
How could he know?
Next thing—
photo shoots
reporters
pampered--
no night hunting here

Owly cocktails
and tasty mice served up—
Little owl could get used
to this fancy treatment.

But no,
they take him home.

That's OK.
Got wings.
Fly back under cover of night
without the press in your face
Maybe even
hang out in that big old tree
just for old time's sake.

Hope

In less than two weeks—just like that
three loved ones are gone.
Too much, too soon for tears
just grey overcast,
stunned souls
and darkness.

Rain mocks our lack of crying,
continues for days, a dripping dirge,
when out of the corner one day a splash—
hundreds of miniature suns
burst from the forsythia bush.
I call to Claudia, "Come see, come see!"
There is lightness,
Resurrection

Missed Opportunity

Pearl visits via dragonfly avatar
I am watering the garden
and stop to snap a photo, but that's it
I don't even say "hello."
Pearl sighs, "Not much has changed. Still
preoccupied with his this and that."

I catch a sense, read her thoughts,
drop the hose and walk to the hosta
but she has already gone
visiting others more receptive

Sheets

Ghosts in the garden,
old torn sheets, like spirit skin,
skeletons, not of bone
but pepper plants, basil, toad lilies
impatiens, Japanese painted fern
like ancestors assembled
for Memorial Day weekend—my mother
Pearl, her farmhand touch,
Morinobu's and Kiyoshi's eye for color
Ume's hunchback patience
And me, gardener watching the sky
for frost to leave before I plant
more immigrants in the established bed
of wild ginger, hosta and iris
I wonder at the unseasonable weather. These
seasons in chaos a test for what can grow
in a ghost prairie

The Skies of Glasgow

Oh multitudes of pigeons,
seagulls rule here.
Claim the air
in the glens of pedestrian malls
and bully you for bits of tourist droppings.
Oh they swoop and swerve
riding the currents of air
like skateboarders on the half pipe
If you can't do tricks with them,
best you don't mess around.

Visitors

It is miracle enough
this volunteer great blue lobelia
surveying the mixed columbine
and garden phlox
Stretching up near the side fence
to the gardener's delight.
And three more sprouts in the
garden path await sunnier digs.

With the shoots safely planted,
the gardener will remember
the resiliency of a
seemingly fragile life—
How it takes root, holds
to new ground—
Hope renewed.

Waiting for the Monarchs

The stage is set as
milkweed snaps open
pink popcorn balls.
Butterfly weed, liatris
stretch sunward, and
Michigan lilies droop
become jester caps
Coneflowers blink out
petals of rose, mustard
and faded chalk

The gardener, neither hopeful,
nor impatient,
worries the underside of leaves
for the white dot signaling
a monarch's beginning.
Worries too, about
reports of a late cold snap
and snow in Mexico.
How many survivors?
How many strong enough
To make the long journey north?
How many to show their finery
On the stage of his garden?

Consider the Lilies...

Yes, and consider the snowdrop, Turkmani
tulip, tongues of crocus pushing through
the last of the snow. Consider the yellow
bellwort nodding its head in the evening spring
or the Canadian violets startling the breeze with
their purple inking open beside the Japanese painted fern,
meadow rue and columbine.
They all create a garden where just last week lay barren dirt.
Consider each blooming miracle— The spiral code
within each seed, each corm and snoozing rootstock

I call myself a gardener but realize
I have done nothing. Soon, I'll weed, mulch,
feed and water, but this first emerging will stay a mystery
So why should I worry about my small life
When I am here in the garden?

EARTH AND SKY

April Fools

Well, it's Minnesota
What do you expect?
Rain, sleet, thunderstorm,
slush and snow—sure, but all at the same time?

What do you expect?
It's Minnesota!
Would I hope for snowdrop
buds popping open
white eyelids to spring sun
or crocus bursting out with royal hues?
The optimistic gardener imagines
Turkmani tulips
Siberian iris,
But no...

It's Minnesota
What do you expect?
Outdoor home-openers at risk
The Twins, the Loons are on their benches
Shaking fists at the sky

Drought

The landscape thirsts
Big bluestem puffs out seed heads early
but smaller, like their lesser cousins.
Ironweed blooms are gone in a day.
Conifers rain needles on the lawn and sidewalk,
a poor substitute for the real thing

Birds sense limitations too,
fighting for a spot at the feeder
budging in the birdbath

Is this the way it is now?
Water rationing and the AC on all night
Forest fires have gone out of control,
making their own weather.
Our nights disturbed by worry.

First Snow

The sky is a watercolor wash
Grey, white, with a ghost of blue beneath
God shakes lower cumulus clouds
Flakes hit the pavement—
a film of mild discomfort
Harbinger of times to come

Time now to trim the garden to its winter flat-top
Bring in the geraniums and hibiscus
Harvest the last of the peppers
Any un-wilted basil?
Put up the fairy lights at least
before finger-numbing nights

Time now
hang out on the porch, late afternoon
suck in as much sunlight as one can
and release it slowly in the dark months.

Flood Stage

Mallards paddle
where furrowed fields should be.
The St. Croix and Missssissippi
lap at foundations and stoops.
There's either way too much
Or not enough—
No meeting in the middle

Is the climate mocking
our politics—giving
no middle ground,
just extremes?

Or is it the other way around—
The grid-locked political climate
forcing the extremes in the global climate?

Flying Over Greenland

Dragons' jaws rip at the sky
Icy inlets quench mountain fire
A wild and wonderous place
Where if you search for dragons
You can miss the land

Flying to L.A.

The Sierra Nevada pounces
at the sky as if
the peaks could be alto-cumulus
It won't work.
Roots too far down, too much history as rock
to be sky material.
So, they are caught
Halfway between—
heads in the clouds,
feet still locked deep
in rocks' stories.

Leaving Black Friday

We are leaving Black Friday
The crowded stores just more COVID havens
and traffic jams of folks cooped up to long

Computers put to sleep
Sunny day, and a car on the road
Wisconsin highway thirty-five
St. Croix River on our right
Winding afternoon light
Stubbled fields gleam
brass and copper as shadows grow

Aspen and birch metallic too
bare branches platinum and pewter
against bottle brush background
and limestone bluffs
We leave Black Friday in the rearview mirror
On the road to the meaning of the season

Weather in Retrograde

April turns into March
Then into February
And the school kids get out of whack
parkas over their shorts
and flip-flops
Teachers feel the natural order upset, get ornery,
Snap at mundane misbehavior
Put off correcting math homework
Wish for Martinis on the porch

It's worse for the gardeners.
Annuals put in too early are toast,
and what about the blooms to come--
frostbite on magnolia, forsythia and azalea?

Boss Robin gives me a cock-eyed look
As if this is all my fault
What part of my actions or inactions
cause turbulent weather?

Wonder

It is unbelievable
Cosmic wonder
The moon exactly the right size
to blot out the disc of the sun
But just as amazing
Hundreds of teens
Eyes skyward
Not on their devices
Not checking each other's TikTok moves
Not texting
Just wide-eyed

This is awe, not contrived "awesome"
This is the real deal
In real time
Not Photoshopped, AI enhanced
No wonder they burst into cheers
Something bigger than themselves,
Taylor Swift, Beyonce, Usher
Something they will remember
They will tell their kids
"I was there. I really saw it."
Showing the pictures they took
on their own iPhones
So the children of the children

will take their own eclipse day off
Travel cross-country
on a path to totality

HOMO SAPIENS

Dark Christmas

There is no Christmas this year in Bethlehem
No star of wonder burning bright, but flares
and tracer bullets--even the inn is closed
and boarded up. What now for the young couple?

They join the ranks of people wandering the street
Looking for shelter while Netanyahu out-Herods
Herod. Not satisfied with infants under
three, he kills everyone in his way.

"What is the line between defense and terrorism?"
The young woman wonders.
How is annihilating an entire country a defensive act?

The terrorists killed 1,200 and kidnapped 240, OK, a
very bad thing
But killing over 50,000 non-combatants in return
makes a joke:
An eye for an eye?

Mary ponders all these things in her heart
Wonders why God would become human
in the midst of all this? And not just this one place,
everywhere it seems, disruption, chaos and destruction--
Even nature itself reveals its Kali side

Her water breaks
Joseph frantically searches for a safe place
Settling on an abandoned Toyota pickup.
Not a manger with fresh hay, a charred vinyl seat
The welcoming bed for the new child

And then Mary understands
This world out of joint, the clash of brother on brother
The greed for power, the neglect of the needy
Is the reason God has come to earth

She recalls someone saying hope--
Not the wimpy sentiment,
but muscular, resisting, rising to action hope
A non-violent insurgency
So much to ask of in an infant, in any one human
She looks up at the smoke-filled sky
and finds she is humming a melody, centuries old,
A new Magnificat

Gone

–for Jim Smith, 1-12-2023

We remember your wry humor
How you found irony in politics—
Metaphors for aging,
How you made the perfect Martini
Shaken, not stirred
Measuring so carefully
With your medical beaker

We remember how you sparked
our conversations, your historical insight
and literary savvy—you were
rarely shaken, but often stirred.
Measured over years.

And now we remember
we all had plans
for after COVID—for after the stroke
until you vanished,
leaving us shaken and stirred
Measuring our lives against yours

Jesus Weeps over the City

Jesus wept as he looked
over Washington D.C.
"Oh you have turned the place
of hope into a place of spite
Even the holiest of buildings—
the building of the people,
damaged by the people it serves.

Oh Washington, named for
a flawed visionary
You have focused on the flaws
and not the vision

This place, where prophets
are scorned
and liars are exalted
I fear, yes for myself
and more, for all my children."

Land Steward

Ian knows every tree on the land
from redwood, beech, hazel.
He knows their age
where they have come from, and what happens
when you clear-cut the landscape, the succession
of flora and fauna that will fill the void

Here, he is master and commander
wisdom in muddy boots
He plans planting and harvests,
does damage control
Thins the herds of deer, seeks
evidence of wild boar

He tells stories rocks and grasses keep
to themselves--interprets the lyrics
of thrush songs and sparrows chirps
Yet he would have us see
A simple man

Letter to My ELL Teacher

Look at this!
Here I am writing
Writing English
Not Spanglish
Not half this, half that
Oh my mami's eyes
will sparkle like Christmas tree
Lights all over the house
To see this

When I came here
I was a real scaredy wuss
(see, I learned kid language too)
NO one to talk to
Well, my kid brother
But who wants to just talk
With a second grader
And nobody else?

Teacher, oh she is nice
Sometimes too nice
Talking to me like
I am second grade
Like my brother
Nice, but not really
Getting me

So then I come to your class
everyone shy at first
But then you—
You really understand me
Like you crossed
The border check-point
Holding my hand

And so pretty soon
We are singing and playing
games and puzzles
How is that learning? Mami wonders
But I know better
Every time, more words come out
Stick in my head like magnet poem

Masks Off!...

And folks are giddy like
Kindergarteners with a snow day
masks fly off faces
into the trash bin like fall leaves
But I am still leery.
It's not as if COVID has given up
As if folks don't die every day

Masks have become habits
A mini-security blanket
I feel odd,
unsafe without them
fogging my glasses
cutting airflow—
An inconvenience like armor

What We Know

–for Rob McIlrath 6-6-2022

What we know is that he
was a quiet, gentle man
who wrestled with demons,
who sometimes won,
and sometimes didn't
but bounced back

What we know is that he
cared about fir trees
birch, tall grass and coneflowers
while working inside brick and glass

What we know is that he
did not talk much
But when he did,
it was with wisdom
thought, and yes,
a wry humor

What we know is that he
wrapped his wife, his step-kids
their families
in a great bear hug

What we know is that he
enjoyed the life of the mind
Books and words
and more books and words
The enjoyment of the hunt
for knowledge
more than the knowing

What we know is that he
was a plain–clothes man
no fancy-schmancy stuff for him
though he could clean up real nice
if the occasion demanded

What we know is that he
took himself away
in the quiet of the morning
Took himself far enough
so his death would not mark the place
cherished—
the work of hearts and minds and sweat
The place of creation.

What we know is that he
had no idea how much
he mingled in our marrow
in our wondering at the stars,
in our songs around the great fires.

He will be remembered
in pathways through the woods,
the springtime nova of the prairie,
the hidden currents of the river,
the call of the Redwing Blackbird by the road,
mud and gravel that sticks between our toes

MEMORIAL

The step-children imagine a memorial
A pathway cut into the tall prairie
Winding to a shrine, a place on the earth
to mark with Rob

I wonder its necessity—
This place, the farm
already holds the spirit of the man
The arching-birdsfoot seedheads of Big Bluestem
The spreading Indian grass,
bottle gentian and coneflower
All full of the quiet reflection of Rob
and across the path, saplings
gown mature buffering the land he loved
from motorcycle buzzing, weekend traffic from the cities

Listen to the wind through the tall grass
The aspen and pine
Can you hear it?
Rob's twinkling laugh, he's getting ready
to crack a joke,
put everything in perspective

A CHRISTMAS CAROL ("...SLEEP IN HEAVENLY PEACE"...)

Doug, you give us a paradox
You are still with us,
yet we cannot go where you have gone
For you are in the heart of love and wisdom
that is God
We all will follow in our own time
but for now, your spirit
infuses us all

We try to recall your seemingly
simple technical fixes
Remember your wry (yes, sometimes snarky) humor
Your gentle, confident wisdom
And most of all, your camaraderie
and love of children

Oh the children!
May your spirit stay with us now
Especially in this time of grief
To remind us
That this is the season of the returning of the light
The children, our charges, and our hope
Will feel your ghost within them
Opening their eyes to wonder

… and Then She Wasn't

She was there waving in a posting
from a hospital bed
Then she was gone
COVID
We have all relaxed
The pandemic over
But the micro-organism
is opportunistic
finds a door not locked,
a window cracked
and steals inside.
Too late, too late
comes recognition
Too late, too late
secondary infections
take over
Too late, too late
We comprehend
The bug is not done with us.

MISSING PRESENCE

April 6, 2024 for Claudia Cannon

Garden plots all up and down
and around Queen Anne Hill
pout, worry, grow anxious--
the hand that clears the mulch,
pulls the early weeds,
waters and feeds the blinking
heads of crocus and tulips
is late.

"What is the matter?" they mumble
across the back yard and boulevards.
"She is always so prompt
and careful."
"What is with her?" they grumble.

The news comes on the wind--
the chatter of grossbeak and sparrow
The Gardener is gone. The careful hand,
the observant eye, the thoughtful mind
all back to ash.
The buds blink once in disbelief
and again in comprehension
As all over Seattle, gardens,
like the gardener
go dormant

Openings

The high school class is like a magnolia bud
Apparent, but mute
The teacher waits
Patient, cajoling
Patient, cajoling
A gardener with hose
Feeding, then waiting
And slowly, the petals unfold
Bit by bit revealing
Inner beauty
A word, a thought
Who knows what the trigger?
They bloom with stories
Stories, and more.

Homeless Camper in Glasgow

It is not lost on us
In the shadow of Marks and Spencer's
toney goods, luscious groceries
we encounter a pad, a sleeping bag
a lump—vaguely human in form—

Someone who sleeps off the day unless roused
by a jangle of change in a chipped mug
or a visit from Social Services
Necessary questions asked

But at night
pals arrive, debate the shit
of the world, their lives
serenade the wakeful tourists
at three in the morning
The sun rises to quiet streets
Early shopkeepers stepping briskly
around the lumpy encampment of one

Salade Niçoise

I could say it was the dish that wooed me
A man who doesn't expect roast beef and potatoes
waiting for him at 5:15, sharp
But one who makes the meal, serves it up
with a bit of flourish
Perhaps that was a part of the wooing?
Always in the Ken and Pat bowl
the jade-green celadon one with the iris
carved into the bottom

Always tuna, though now it is from jars
Imported from Italy instead of the hockey puck tin
oil-filled casket for Charlie.
And potatoes, boiled egg, red onion, anchovies,
olives
There are variables: green beans or asparagus? Capers?
Little bell peppers and cherry tomatoes?
But always, always lemon juice, not vinegar
And Romaine, though red leaf is OK.
Preferable—and a chilled Tavel
Though it seems these days a Spanish Garnacha
catches the same light on the tongue
This tradition
started the beginning of togetherness

Stamps

for Mick Uphoff. 1946—2022

Bob and Ginny return from San Diego
with Mick's remembrances
A Michael Daly painting, of course
But what's this? A Stamp collection?
We thought we knew all about Mick
But stamps? That's a new one!

Making piles by categories—
Countries, people, wildlife,
reveal a deep affection
for what we could only skim in conversations
Stamps for baseball and Olympic sports
Stamps commemorating--
Patricia Harris, Martin Luther King, Roy Wilkins and
Malcom X

In another pile: Billy Mitchel, Omar Bradley, John L.
Hines, Harry Truman
Yet another: Grace Kelly, Max Steiner, Frida Kahlo,
Leonard Bernstein, James Dean,
Louise Nevelson, Richie Valens, Ayn Rand

Clearly, we have underestimated Mick
Through these stamps we see a picture we lost
over the distances via posts from

Japan, Canada, Australia, the Cayman Islands,
Sweden, Poland, Ukraine—

His correspondents--
What stories would they share
of our gardening, hair stylist, summer celebrant,
fierce friend?

Steps

How many steps
Did it take to get here—
English muffins, pepper jelly,
boiled egg, bowls of berries,
strong coffee?

Do we start counting the steps
from that first February afternoon
We mingled our belongings
Piled into "La Casa del Rio Zumbro"?

How many steps
to reading in bed at night
You interrupting—"Listen to this"
Or me reading aloud a Joy Harjo poem?

Do we start counting steps from
South Chicago—the U.P.

How many steps
To singing for neighbors
on the porch, and then
neighbors online, livestreamed
Bob Dylan filtered through me,
The third-generation Japanese
boy imagining Neil Young?

Do we start with grandfather's
steps up the gangplank
to the steamer heading
for the land of dreams,
or the steps of flight of your ancestors
away from the rampages
of the British army after Culloden?

How many steps to this young baby boy
fifth of the great-grandkids
taking you into his world-view?

Or do we start with the steps
of a newly evolved walking fish—
the first hominid peering
into the future in a new sunrise?

Teacher Appreciation, 5-2-2022

Teachers,
You may have an inkling
but it is just that--
how your magic ripples out
how many lives you change for the better
Even lives not yet breathing on this earth

You may have a feeling
a sense
of the opening you instigate
every day, invasions
of knowledge and imagination exchanged
between you and your students' minds

You may know a bit
but not the fullness of all
who give you thanks
every minute the earth still turns
for your gift most wondrous

Teacher Workshop Week

Even though it is not my place anymore
I am anxious, full of anticipation—
still have that adrenaline rush
of the new and unexpected
this week of preparation
re-bonding with the teacher teams

An odd feeling--being the spectator
at a distance
not in small groups
bitching about new changes,
comparing notes about students,
thinking up new ways
to make the room welcoming.

Yet I do worry about the teachers
How they will adjust and cope
with life in flux
within the schools
The world outside the sanctuary
full of uncertainly
and dangers.
Will resilience of minds and young bodies
be enough to counter
the pressures?

Teachers
like jazz soloists
fill the melody to the fullest
but improvise on a moment's whim

Will they carry on
In the greater Suite
where before was cacophony?
Let it swirl to create a wonderous song!

The Kids Won't Let Go

Just when you think they have forgotten,
don't care
there is a post, an email
"Friend" request
Still longing for what was
as they move into more uncertainty

The classroom was their safety zone
where they didn't have to be "good students,"
just themselves with their thoughts and fears
and ways of showing they got it—

where what was important
was not the lesson plan.

THE LIFE WITHIN

This husk,
skin and bones
is not your brother
The growing up secret stories
laughs and tantrums
do not live inside

The voice that questioned,
and cajoled,
and whispered
like a breeze through the high pines
does not live here either

Nor do all the actions
interactions
late night worries
and daylight horseplay
that pass between siblings

You do not need the white pages
to look your brother up
The address is the heart's center,
or the house of spirit.

The Queen Is Dead…

Long may she live
not in arguments about constitutional monarchy
Or royals versus commoners
She was a fixture of my time,
crowned the year I was born
The first queen of the TV age,
The media age,
Internet—
She spanned the generations
From newsprint to Tik Tok
From jazz to hip-hop
All the time upon a throne
a very human woman
Her voice, her celebrations and failures
Known around the globe
We knew her better than any textbook monarch
And so I lift a glass
Not to the position
But to Elizabeth, a girl thrown
into history and a niche
in my marrow bone
Long may she live

The Words Remain

–for Hardy Coleman

You'd see him and imagine him
one of the vagabonds at Woodstock
reveling in the weed and rain and music
Maybe writing a song about it all

You might even see him in a prison cell
composing sonnets and quatrains
to pass the time, amuse himself
Maybe writing a song about it all

You might see him on a ladder
hammer in hand, nails pinched in his lips,
tacking up drywall or hacking out dry rot
Singing a song about it all

You want to see him in front of a mic
threading tales in and out of each other
bound in the cadence of poetry
Becoming a song about it all

Life and death--the muck of it
The voice now still
but words becoming music
in our hearts and minds –a song of Hardy

Waiting (Again) Gonda Building

At the Mayo Clinic a wall of glass
becomes a giant video screen
The set pieces,
the Kahler Hotel and Plummer Building

The woman in shades and faux-fur coat
saunters towards the revolving doors--
delaying a test result?

Storefronts deprived of sunlight,
this play is not a detective thriller
but may be a melodrama
the plot written by shifting light,
the plodding gait of time
a world waiting for its fever to break

Where Are the Answers?

She talks about self-harming
matter of fact—the weather report,
a football score.
Why is it a topic of daily discourse?

Taking the easy way out,
we say, "Oh it's all a product of the pandemic,
the isolation, lack of contact"
But that is only the torn corner of a snapshot
We lose the big cinematic picture. Our denial?

Plenty of reasons for her depression.
How about how we fucked up the planet,
or how we let despots run the world—
everything with a dollar sign attached
We elect small minds with gorged egos

And we let them wreck the lives of women,
mess up the minds of children,
and disregard the promises we all made
This will be the first generation that has not
been more successful than its forebears

The first generation to see the possibility
it might not see another generation following

The first generation to understand
Homo Sapiens are not the dominant species

While we moan about this and that
And career politicians sit on their asses and
spew their crap into an already toxic atmosphere
the world rolls on towards oblivion
She and her peers seemingly alone
See a dark tide rolling.

Prom Night

Back in the day, Prom Night
was a big deal—just me and my date
Eddie Websters, The Normandy.
If you were really fancy,
Charlie's Café Exceptionale
or the Rosewood Room,
And heaven forbid if anyone you knew
showed up at the same venue—
cramping your style,
making awkward even more so.

Nowadays, the high schoolers travel in packs
hard to tell if there are any real "dates" or not
taking over entire sections of a burger joint
tables of young women dressed to the tens
a few suits on the guys, but more than a few billed caps
turned backwards
not so much one-to-one romance
as group hugs.
Nowadays, the high schoolers not sure
they will even go to the dance.
Close dancing gone with the COVID shutdown
They have no collective memory of the moves,
the intimacy of hand on waist,
hand on shoulder—
moving in time together

I suppose if you don't know what you missed,
you don't miss it
Yet I feel sorry that these youngsters
won't have the memories I play back
on my internal Netflix
A real band, not some DJ from who knows where
A darkened room, swaying bodies
Yes, even the faculty and parent chaperones
to keep in check raging hormones

A rite of passage like so many others
these young people will never know

The Philadelphia 11 – Film Screening, May 14, 2024

It was fifty years ago—
Could have been today.
So aggravating
that women still have to fight
to be in control of their lives,
their bodies,
their life path

Men of fear
push their thumbs down
even more now
that women, en masse,
scale the rock face
created by power, greed and misconception

Men of fear
deny real changes
all around them—
cowering in their strongholds
making pronouncements from their bunkers
unable to accept the new world order

Men and Women of courage
push through the doorways
clear new pathways

Embrace a world
where everyone
lives with meaning and purpose

WEE POEMS FROM SKYE

Wee Poems From Skye

1. Time Shift

The light is golden on the locust tree
The light I love for taking pictures
Writing poems,
A four-in-the-afternoon
on the porch
kind of light
Except here it is ten minutes after nine
bodies thinking it is time for bed
but the eyes say
"Must stay awake,
take as much as you can
of this light, this time."

2. Skye, From Gaellic

"Sgiath" meaning wing
the winged isle
that takes us to the sky
everywhere, our eyes turn upward,
a spirit, a force in the rocky earth,
the heaven pointing Cuillins
Even the lochs are filled with sky

3. Sheep…

… here on Skye amble
like schoolkids
no rush, a vague direction
But steady on
Perhaps the reason
Scotland has the rule of passage
Through any parcel of land
Sheep in the middle of the road
A single track traffic jam

4. The Ruined Castle, Duntuln

Could this be where Agatha, "the Good Hawk"
Stood watch? These stones, the stones she walked?
These walls, where she sounded the alarm?

The scenes flash
Like movies on the screen of the world
As big as the heavens of Skye
As big as a young woman's imaginings

5. Armadale

See-through castle
Open to mists
Grand stairway to nothing—
facade holding only ghosts
Man's ambition in ruins

6. In Place at Last

The mist descends
And the mountains clutch it
With their jagged teeth
Wringing out the rain.
We thought Minnesota summer
Had followed us
But Scotland returns

FRESH SIGHTINGS

It has been a tradition in many societies for the mentor to include the work of student/proteges in their own work. I continue that tradition here with the work of former students who have generously (and bravely) shared their work. Look for them and their own books/creations in the not-too-distant future! (Students retain the copyright to their work!)

CASSIE KLUESS

Time's Bind

–for TG

If I could journey into the past
Find you
Before you'd walked experience's path,
Before you lost your way
In a starless haze
I would let you know
That I believe,
I'd dare you to dream
Take your hand & lead you
To the future
through the past,
Show you the stars
& everything they are
How they make up you
& everything you do
I wouldn't leave
Not until you believed
In you
& while I'd lose you in the future
From rewriting the past
I'd be so relieved
Knowing you found relief

In your younger days
& experienced the fullness of life
Before the gray could ever come your way.

Skygazing

In the daytime
The stars hang overhead
Yet it's hard to believe, isn't it?
While they can't be seen
Between the sun & clouds
That they're up there
Dreaming

Unexpected Company

The moon says "hi"
From the early morning sky
& I can't help but wish
To stay in its presence
As long as I can
Cherishing its unexpected company
In the early morning rise

JAMIE COZIK

Church Pews

She showed a side of her heart
That shattered with every beat
The ice-cold blood it pumped
Was the reason she was so mean

She once had a smile that no one could touch,
Until the pain became all too much
Now muddled with hurt and deceit,
Her soul heard a darker drumbeat

Her heart tormented, she could take no more
No matter her path, she'd been led to locked doors
She's lost, what is there left to do?
She asks herself, *is anything true?*

Now everyone she ever knew
Sits around her in church pews.

LILLY HEWITT

Good Ol' Days

Sitting on a creaky rocking chair
My hair turning a brownish reddish gray
Wrinkles decorate my face and hands
Smile lines dot the corners of my mouth
From many moments of laughter

My grandchildren sitting criss cross applesauce
Laughing at my stories
Their questions burning in their mouths
There's something sweet in the oven
It's aroma filling the living room

I imagine recounting this time in my life
The rollercoaster of teenage girlhood
I heard a quote once
"We never know we're in the good o
Ol' days
Until we've passed them"

I feel as if I'm on the cusp of them
Like a sunrise after a forever night
Like sisyphus finally rolling up that boulder
Looking back on who I was even 9 months ago
Is like staring back at a stranger

Everyone comments on my change
Whether it's the lost pounds or the lost baggage
"What diet are you on?"
"Your attitude is so different now!"
Seem to dance freely from my peer's lips

The best compliments come from my own
Grandmother
"You've turned your life around, Bean"
"You look so confident, Bean"
"My beautiful Bean"
I hope to make my granddaughter feel this way someday

The world now looks as if God turned up the saturation
And so I thank Him for allowing me to finally see it

Enough

Is my mascara too clumpy?
Is my hair too frizzy? A stain on my clothes?
Is it my double chin? The hump on my nose?
Is it my painfully average face or my squishy body?
Am I not pretty enough for my phone to light up?

Do I talk too much? Am I too odd?
I'm scared of taking up too much space
Am I not saying all the right things?

I think you can smell the desperation I reek of
Is there a reason I feel like the last pick in dodgeball?

Watching my friends getting hit on and flirted with
Wondering if I look either too gay, intimidating, ugly
Or all of the above
After years, I've finally found my confidence
But why do I still not feel like I'm enough?

I look in the mirror and feel pretty sometimes
My big brown eyes, wavy hair, small rib cage
But I feel like my eyes are playing tricks on me
Because how can I look like this
And have none of the attention I crave?

I pause my homework, my tv shows, just to respond
Like the next coat of lipgloss will finally make him say something
As if the right picture will make him believe I'm enough
I preach about how we as women should raise our standards
As I eat up the bare minimum like I haven't had a meal in weeks

If romantic affirmation is a drug, I need to be in rehab
If wanting it so bad was a crime, I'm a felon

I know deep down, this obsession isn't good for anyone
But in these months, the adrenaline rush keeps me going
It makes me feel for a moment, I might be enough

Simplified

There seems to be a phenomenon going around
Clique lines and lunch tables suddenly blurred
People I thought hated me flashing a grin
The popular girl sends me a follow request
Its like elementary school again, simplified

People are apologizing, making amends
Signing the yearbooks of those they haven't spoken to in years
HAGS turns into "best luck in the future"
Quick smiles turns into hugs, waves to fighting tears
It's so simple when we know we won't see each other again
Some have reached a level of "done" I didn't think possible
I'm guilty of this as I don't press mute on my facial expressions anymore

I'm guilty of this as it takes much less to make me snap this week
I feel the guilt through a lifetime of striving to be kind
Why can't it just be simple to be a fellow human being?
As we rehearse graduation I feel the weight lifted off me
I am only going to miss a handful of these names
I can look in the mirror and say I didn't reach my full potential
I'd rather weather the storm than only experience a breeze
I'd rather have my goodbyes much more simplified

My future seems like jumping off a cliff with no simple bottom
But I'd rather leap and find out than ever look back

KERRIS VAUPEL

The Apple

Adam gave up a rib for me
But I am the pilot of my bones my skin my mind
All of these savage mechanisms
They serve my spark
Not his

I still do not know if I was wrong
But my answer will never change
anytime I have been asked

I'd bite the apple
So I'd no longer be an empty page
My soul made from clips from magazines

I'd bite the apple
So I could hear more
Than nice words
From a pair of pretty blue eyes

I'd bite the apple
Because I have always believed
That the hand that feeds earns to be bitten
When it needs

The apple cannot frighten me
Not when I choose to open my eyes
That is mine

My life can never be written
Just I move my bones
That is mine

All of my tainted muscles
All of the scars on our limbs
All of these wrinkles on faces
This makes up the beauty of being alive

Heart

I once gave my heart to a knight who cared eagerly for me. Held up a shield to protect my tender parts. But now my body is unguarded. I then gave my heart to a seamstress who wrapped me in gold. Sewed up all my cuts and put me out in the world again. And now I'm bleeding. Before I loved a woodworker who built me a new heart. Cut off my strong edges and sanded me down to the bone. I told myself I could never give my pure heart to another. I wished my heart was more than just a muscle. That it could be stopped when I decided not to go on.

Cultivation

Cultivation is the suffered
But it is the working
Producing and extending history

The steamships railroads paper
Machinery textiles spices guns
And stories
All the printing presses
Mismatched timelines
Works we must remind ourselves of are fiction

Breathing tubes and vaccinations
Food dispensers and scarlet letters
Telephone poles and power lines
Bird nests and snake burrows
Daughters turned builders
And sons turned teachers

Teleportation and space travel
Will become what is to be normal
Remember the ones who laid that foundation
The reason we have yet expired

ACKNOWLEDGEMENTS

"Masks Off!" was previously published in the anthology, *Rewilding Hope*, A Publication of the Cracked Walnut Chapter of the League of Minnesota Poets. The League of Minnesota Poets Press (2023)

Thank you, thank you to all who had a hand in this book—the students who bravely submitted their work; my editor in chief and wife, Claudia Daly; generous and firm primary editor, Mary Jo Thompson; and last-pass editor, Barbara Jones; to Michael Kiesow Moore, Liz Weir, and Paula Cisewski for their wonderful words. Thanks to Jay Monroe for yet another fabulous cover.

A special thank you to Norton Stillman for taking a chance with the manuscript that is now in your hands.

Thanks to independent booksellers everywhere with a shout out to Sub Text, Next Chapter Booksellers, Magers & Quinn, Eat My Words, The Irreverent Bookworm, Big Hill Books in the Twin Cities; Zenith Bookstore and the Bookstore at Fitgers in Duluth; and Foxes & Fireflies Booksellers in Superior.

Gratitude also, for the wonderful community of Minnesota writers, the League of MN Poets, Lake Superior Writers, the Loft, Ginger Poets.

photo: Margaret Hasse

About the Author

Stanley Kusunoki has taught creative writing to young people through programs at The Loft, Asian American Renaissance, Intermedia Arts, and S.A.S.E., The Write Place. He was the recipient of a Loft "Asian Inroads" mentorship, and was awarded a MN State Arts board "Cultural Collaboration" grant to create, write and perform "Beringia—The Land Bridge Project" with Ojibwe performance poet Jamison Mahto at Intermedia Arts. He is the former co-host/curator of the Literary Bridges reading series at Next Chapter Booksellers in St. Paul.

Kusunoki most recently was the High Potential Coordinator at Red Oak Elementary School in Shakopee. He lives in Duluth with his wife, Claudia Daly.